IN RED, IN WHITE
© 2017 by Daja Rene

ISBN 9781944082352 print
ISBN 978xxxxxxxxxx electronic

First Edition

Layout by Susan Bond
Edited by Brinda Iyer, Madison Jardine
and Coyote Rooves
Illustrations by Daja Rene
Cover by Isabela DeSousa and Daja Rene

Printed in the United States of America

In Red, In White

by Daja Rene

July 23rd 2013 - July 23rd 2016

When I was fourteen

the apex of love was obvious

I would be in my late 20s with nothing but mismatched socks, worn granny panties, a similar t-shirt, a fridge full of beer and soy milk, a tiny kitchen of my very own, and a boy.

He would be tiredly sprawled like a star on the floor

A linoleum walk of fame

and I would straddle him, Chinese takeout in hand, leaning to feed him, but instead kissing him as I drop noodle on his soft face. We laugh, make love, fade to black.

[Dream cloud pops and snows over A and I, buying crack from a guy named Chicago at 4 a.m. in a parking lot in Fort Lauderdale.]

Cut to a train crash, a broken body

But still music in its' blood

Train stops

She crawls to catch it

Train goes

Cut to an abandoned ship

only two on board

She has the time and means to leave

but she stays to cry to him in his sleep

He is stitched into night terrors and won't wake

And so she stays

Cut to a gas station across from a college campus

He is spending the last of his money on cigarettes and wine

Her commitment to being agreeable and lovely is unkind to herself

Is out of body, out of love for who he could be

If maybe lean wasn't so cheap this week

She waits adeptly in the car while he takes his purchases in

Cut to twenty minutes later, car crashing

Truth stinging in its hinges

Cut to a love doctor untrained to drain bathtub drugs from he who chugs

He wanted to make a casket of that bathtub

She wanted to make a King of that boy

Cut to her deciding how many pills to take before work and after work

She sorts them in a little Victorian pill case she found

She knows what she's doing; she knows:

1 makes her want to be alone and create

2 makes her intimate yet careless

3 makes her easier to get in bed with

She takes one and a half and calls that responsible

She forgets she's taken any and takes two more

Another kind of car crash

Whether ours were woven by hand or chance

it was still magic how our fates fell in love

with the beauty of a ballet but none of the grace

Our arrival was violent

and our athletic hearts

pump

and pump

from the voids from which we thought we held goodness

pump from the rot and back

recycling tonic into toxic

and furious, bloody spittle into surrendering kisses

Our staminas for forgiveness

knew not when to quit

knew not where reason lives

knew not that our truest love takes time

and place

in another time and place

Takes tolls and hold

in the midst of a quieting battle

Love can make a once strong tigress weak

A dunce cap out of teeth

Leave claw marks on the street

Make a dry ghoul bleed

but I think only true love can do that

I think true love can wilt

Without ever coming back

I think that's how we were killed:

With the very weapons we chose

With our very own claws

That furious blood on curious paws

Undressed wounds, no gauze

Sad, tired animals that build their own jails

Swollen tails

act one

Heart nest

Flying colors, good unsteady, a one-time holiday

A thick and immediate onset of ricocheting contact highs

Cedarwood, eyes closed warmly, dry feet

Soul parts

unfolding and breathing in leaps

US BOTH: FRANTIC OVER DISCOVERING OUR BLUE-
PRINTS FOR PARADISE MATCH AND NEED NOT
GATHER MORE DUST. WE GET TO BUILDING IN A
CLUMSY BUT HAPPY MANIA. SMILES FROTH, RUSHED
EXCHANGE OF FIDELTY.]

-- [forthcoming, something forever]

[home, live performance,
heart's theory, college,
a cradle, a bliss, a need]

July 19th 2013

You are the most amazing
person I've met.
   you
   handsome   prophet
   you
   troubled soothsayer
   you
   exiled , dirty angel

collector of

16   mountains on Earth,

Tonight we found out we share the exact same dreams

I do not think we had a first kiss

Not in this life

My mouth cradled

and remembered you

And I know that's crazy since we were only just friends yesterday

but I know I love you

and I've never felt this inspired in my life

You had your own ambience and I know it by heart: charming, bitter, bragging and like honey. Babe, you were the rich man's whiskey. I should not have had you alone.

You are actually the most charming person I can think of. You get to be caustic, dark, loud and overpowering - and still the greatest person in any room. Your soft heart is a secret by which I've been annointed, and your wit and looks are something I've dreamed of. You are the uncallibrated sun dial one passes when touring a famously beautiful home; impressive but off tune, there for show, there to allude the wonderous things it has done and could do, but currently out of service and on display.

I'm here for more than the tour. I could steal you, easily.

July 21st, 2013

You deserve me for thinking that you don't

I want you because I have great affection for things forbidden

grinning stupid

rolling over drunk

reaching for something of which I can't handle

Maybe we should be together forever

In fact, I will love you with everything, hard and heavy

I love into the eleventh hour

You
are every "him"

You
are the war drum
On my side of the bank

You
are all I was looking for
in every song

[every hymn]

[a baby crane, a short dance, light blue to dark blue to purple love, somewhere between a score and the music, a drug and another dance, laughing critics but esteemed, dirty but it gleams, sewn but not seamed]

Early to love, late to leave
Quick to get the tea and toast started for you.
Sorry to go, even when I have to go, and quick to get started on you.

Was unready to love
like I love you now
But I love you now
With all of this body
All of this hair
All of my goodness
My goodness, I love you with all of my truth and all of my joy
With a full and trusting, all-the-way, no-mistakes, long-lazy-day love.
A by-the-sea love, a please-don't-leave love,

I'm so in love with you but

If something went wrong I'd really cry with my lungs like I'm
drowning and fighting
With my gills like I'm gasping for words to tell you
My favorite love I've ever known is your love

I quite like you
But
Especially how you play
With you I make believe and make it come true
When we are the Trojan horses of our dreams
Oh, how we play into drunken stupor and the happiest oblivion
Oh, how we love all the way through, on our tippy toes
Oh, how I love you these days
with all of my gills and all of my lungs and parts and parcels
and hair and body
But listen,
I love you too much to fall out of your heart by mistake or trial
I rather let love and let go
All long hugs and stiff croaks
I'll come undone and let you know

I love you enough to let you go
than to hold on to you

This is the first time you've been upset with me

Your heart actually seems repulsed

that I told you that my romantic personality is Clem

That Chris was my Joel: he taught me to love, be kind, to own responsibilities

But him and I can't be together anymore

Things are done with him but you don't believe me

When the

emptiness of

our   mouths

play

in this   time   of the   setting sun.

24

[candy, movies, a plane that sits four, $80 of Chinese food, Joel, Clem, you, me]

smiles and eyes are permanently
decorated with a reflection

scratching at each other's brainwork

This is all I want

To dine and play and fight with you
May I always

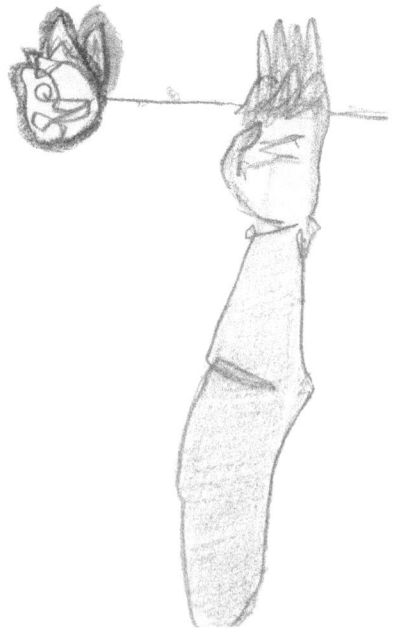

August 1st, 2013

I'm so excited for you to move into my dorm for the fall semester. I could never get sick of you.

But I'm especially excited to change the world with you. All of your book ideas blow my mind.

You're brilliant. I hope you never give up, but just in case, I'll be here to motivate you every step of the way.

Love you, call me when you get home
D x

gills, lungs, to wake up to someone, human, hold

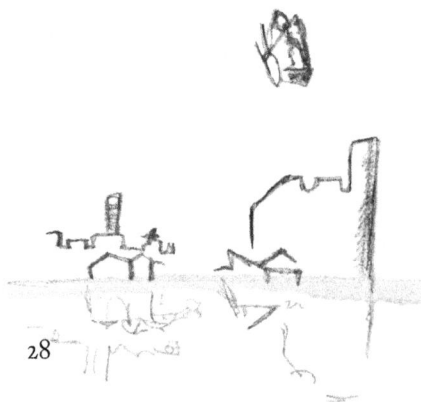

When you fell for me, I was lucky, really very lucky. To have my high school dream boy - the rugged and troubled, witty, writing, raging boy with the good stuff - even hang out with me, I was surely dreaming. And yet you acted bashfully despite knowing your charm captured me.

We figured out what pouring out our hearts meant; to empty it of hurt so there was room to give and receive love again.

So we spilled our minds and their beans, listening eagerly and telling things that were stuck in the back of our heads. We incessantly prattled about our fears, the things we've conquered, our stubborn voids, our peace requiring forgiveness, the invincible ghosts of our invincible dreams, the ghosts of your friends, the reinvention of my heart, our futures, and a little about our pasts. We riled each other up and picked the dust out from under us. We did this all lying on my dorm room floor.

This nervous dance into sacred bond felt bigger than even an idealized version of love; this felt more like magic, in how fast and unbelievably it happened.

When I fell, I got to taking off bandages from the times I fell before. I was healed enough and was only wearing bandages to cover scars I didn't need to any longer.

You were about to help me without judgement, so you deserved to see me, wounds and all. And so you did: you earned, deserved and did away with my pain, stamping a kiss on my hand. I felt the magic throughout.

From the kiss on my hand, to my fingers, to my writings; in my heart and head, and sleep and wake,

where I felt something musical in my blood, something familiar but new, and certain, and promising, and thrilling, and safe.

You felt like finally falling asleep

to the space between not being able to smile, and then doing so.

So we honeymooned my dorm room for eleven days, intoxicated with adoration, until and after reality peaked through like a ray of dusty 6 a.m. light through dusty 2 a.m. blinds.

So we will trip the light fantastic til I prove that I'm for you, always; fall for each other again and again, get used to each other and build each other up after every breakdown, learn each other all over again.

Honey, you are my best friend: I am your dog and you, my diamonds. Odd bird and odd ball, for the long or short haul: can I always have this dance?

You said the rain makes you feel confident. You said, "maybe it is because I can smell and feel the humidity in my once broken bones. Those bones are now twice as strong."

I believe in you so much

[Trojan horse, risk]

Casual divinity:
We spend hours fooling around
arguing over who is luckier to have the other
over which one of us is crazier
This feels like hanging out with God in a bar
how funny and brilliant and unbelievable it all is

[certainty, good shiver, new future]

Let me know where you'd want your wedding to be

I've been trying so hard to be the perfect girlfriend to keep you happy. I don't want our baggage to break open and make a mess so please unpack with me, bit by bit. I can help. I can help. I'll build you up, brick by brick.

I forgive you ahead of time.

You don't have to apologize when a wound reopens. I know you will say sorry anyway.

You don't have to leave angry.

It seems you will anyway.

I love you, please

Let me in to help you

Your girl

August 21st, 2013

Baby, baby, baby.

You had me.

I just walked out, heart in hand, ready to give you my body/
soul, and you looked at me for a good minute and said, "Could
you just take a bunch of selfies on my phone tonight?" I've been
honored to be adored by someone like you, and honored by the
way you would just abruptly hug and hold my face and say, "We
found each other. We're fucking aliens." It became permanent
when I heard you not so secretly cooking for me downstairs.
You came back in quietly, your eyes and focus all on me and
I felt like someone really thought I was beautiful for the first
time. I think young love is real love. I think I'll die with you be-
ing mine. I think fate might be true.

Even with all our trouble and fighting this past month, I
haven't forgotten all the love in our voices when we couldn't
catch a breath. I know these are tests I'm willing to take. See
you later tonight, my love.

[standing on my cape]

My birthmarks and scars don't make a constellation yet

I'm sure no one else saw the rips of a riverbed in your hair

or loved you thoroughly, loved you for all your knots and shame

or loved me through it all, through all I do and have done

If The Fates were woven, the hands of a god somewhere

were distracted by the innocence of two sad faces

braided ours together in a broken lovely twine

so as to knot, twist and pattern in all the right places

[race, red light]

What good are these

Jewels and butterflies

Today you asked me why I "put up" with you. I put up with you because I hope you're well on your way to give me nothing to put up with. Besides, as sharp as your tongue gets after it's tasted benzos, you are otherwise very good to me.

[italicized heart, underlined time, undermined mind, proofread person]

There's a difference between being alone and being left alone; that being whether or not you have anyone to leave you alone at all. And I need you to take it the right way and give me space lovingly, not get angry at me when I ask for space. Give and take. That's what I'd like for us to be about.

As violent as you left, I actually hope you do know you can always come back.

You always justify adding to your headstash; something happened to "I want to get clean for a girl like you."

What happened to that? What happened to the promise to stop serving once you reup one more time, once you're done mourning Alex's death, once you find a job? What happened to finding a job? When I try to remind you of these hopes you hung pretty over our door, you vilify me, turning it around and into something else.

Do you have to call me names to get your point across?

I am not a 'child'

or a 'coward'

or a 'flirt'

August 14, 2013

I think we can substitute some drugs for some art. Everything you've been taking is taking a toll on your sense of self, while creative energy sustains and waters that sense of self.

You come off as invincible when you use
- you can function, carry decent conversations about things you like to talk about, things you are good at,
things
like
that.
But this isn't to say your personality is not impaired.

I've been afraid to bring this up to you because I didn't want you to be done with me (the way you always are, whenever I suggest you take less of anything). What you don't see is that you could take something else and still have the same stimulation and relish you seek; you can take to writing more, take to painting again, to cooking more often. I would not get in the way of that.

I am not saying quit doing drugs; obviously we have fun and they make you money. But I tell you first hand, honestly and carefully, that I get scared when you have delusional fits from drinking that green syrup or smoked those "80s". I don't even really know what those are, but hate them, because they make you mean. Same goes for when you take three or more sticks.

The version of you I fell for doesn't put his money and his drugs first; the day I fell in love with you, you were actually sober: bright and ambitious, peaceful and productive with the time to talk to me, to look me in the eye, to laugh with me and talk about all the hope we've got, all the love we're coming up on. That's why I beg you to come to bed and relax - so we could maybe revisit that space. But these past few months, you insist on frantically recounting your money at your desk between lines of bars.

["I miss you"]

Cut to two months later, a contract was started on an iPhone 3G

I'll efficiently straighten up your room for every time you take a 25 minute walk with me.

I'll put your clothes away for every time you write with me.

I won't ask for anything for Christmas if you stop doing Xanax for good.

Nov 1, 2014

To Do With You

make sand castles
kidnap a mutual friend
go to CB Smith
get hypnotized professionally
take pictures of each other on film
make special cake and bring it to the movies at midnight in our
pajamas with Valium and wine and a big soft Asian blanket
Climb huge tree

I'm not sure how you think
you can push me away
with self pity

I don't ask for much
but all I'm asking now
is that you don't make me beg you
to come to bed to
let me make you feel better

all I'm asking now
is that you cut back so that we can talk at night
at least a few nights a week
[I am willing to compromise]
cut back so that we can sell more than we take
so that you don't say things to me that you don't mean

if you really want to push me away
if you want me to leave
you will have to make me

[drums, chest]
 [drugs, tests]

My favorite feeling in the universe is being on the same high
as you

Two bars, one superman, and a line

Last night was perfect

You said to me, "You shouldn't have to hide your knives from me." Somehow I argued, and now I'm more sorry now that you're high about it. You're distancing yourself when I just want to be your bath time.

I adore you to where your favorite songs and books are very important to me, sometimes more important than my favorite songs and books. The same goes for your happiness. I think I have been so focused in seeming happy to give you less to worry about that something builds up in me, snapping when it gets the chance.

After I mess up and you still stay, I am always overwhelmed with guilt and gratitude and unwillingness to let you go. I'm filled with the feeling of "let's go home", but then we're here; you are home, family, everything and all I need.

A void in me craves you infinitely - your serif curls and all your demons. And marriage may not satisfy that void but it is the best thing I can think of. And I know we didn't believe in marriage but look at how we dream now. Look at how we've kicked the fear of slowing to a rut, trusting that although old marriage may not be as thrilling as what we chase these days, it is still many other things love wants to be when it grows up.

[karmic angel, insomniac, depend, spirit of it, fever of it, soft wife]

Nothing I show you is for show

why you think otherwise, I don't know

But I've no time for the run and go

of loving you insincerely

When clearly

your nightly embrace is the silence of snow

You have me

feel like a soup

of nicotine

that hits like candy

This is how

you make me believe

your claim

that I'm as invincible as elementary school dreams

I'm sorry that I don't remember last night

You said I threw my new glass ring holder and my
roommates left

That I screamed as though I was being tortured
All the way till you left

The passion of this
honeymoon won't
expire in due course
or be withered by these
Let me
in and on to marry you
Fix all your fixing and
devotedly love all
of your hurt

Dear, I am so bound;
I want to be your
remedy and I'd
hope my heart's flooding
affection
shows

Look through my things
please
For I've been loyal and making lists
of my dreams
and big schemes
counting the lashes
in your loving eyes, I wouldn't mind
growing up
to spend my life reading you
a colosseum of libraries
a warm wind over cold puddles
pinwheel heart, moonbeams pour
into each of our pores

You are the war drum
Just across the water

Discover holy, discover angels, faraway messages, priests, angels,

proximity of a God, window of light, sun, yellowish,

Compatible strengths

and heartstring and brain wave length

I'll love you summer to summer easily

You bring up the people I've slept with before you

I'm ashamed and feeling dirty after the interrogation

Like soap and skin,

I've tried every day to undo and refresh

I am still the same page

There is still inkling left

and such is to come

I am not that person

I'm sorry other men met my body before I met you

but I cannot change that

still, you're cold about it

August 14, 2013

I made it 3 days sober

until last night

to which you said,

"it doesn't count as a relapse because you don't have a problem,"

to which I said

nothing

August 15, 2013

I thought Xanax was supposed to make you tired. It used to make me tired but last night I couldn't sleep.

Prior to staying up until 7:15 a.m., I went downstairs for some tea and got caught cuddling with Jalex on your dining room floor by your mother, which suprisingly led to us bonding. She begged me to eat, claiming that I never do. We talked about why she doesn't mind me living here, and why she is heartbroken over what you think of her.

She goes, "I don't get why the hell he's always so angry! Of course he's been through hell, but so have we! And we forgave him because we love him so much!" Now she was trying really hard to not cry. "But why can't he forgive us? He always brings up our past and our old problems but all we want is for us to move forward! He always thinks we're bringing him down but we just want him to really be his best, which is so, so much!"

Long, awkward, sad silence was made comfortable by Jalex having another fit. But the fact that there wasn't much more to say kept it awkward enough for me to come upstairs with a lot on my mind.

[night terror, a plane, your dealer, your dealer's daughter, bad
medicine]

act two

[battle royale, love-lorn,
looping, one or several,
little wounds]

[BOY: STRINGING AXIOMS AROUND THE HOUSE. VERY MATTER OF FACT, VERY TO THE POINT. ONE SAYS, "YOU HAVE TO FIGHT FOR ME IF YOU EVEN CARE AT ALL." THE NEXT DAY, HE TAKES THIS ONE DOWN, CLAIMING TO NOT REMEMBER HANGING IT.]

[GIRL: SINGING THE BOY DOWN FROM THE STOOL ...]

"So let's make this right. Let me show you your strengths and pet you all over. And won't you look at what wrote for you. And won't you say more than two words about it. And won't you let me in every time. See, I'll bring my broken rhymes, you your meds and Jewish wine, and we can go to sleep at peace this time."

Spring 2014:

Cut to a dorm room designed for two students but only occupying one. Half of the room is arranged for a female student, the other half with boys clothing and tiny baggies strewn all over floor. In the middle of the room sits a scale.

[GIRL: THROWING HER ART AT THE BOY, SCREAMING WITH HER ENTIRE BODY.]

[BOY: BEGGING HER TO RELAX.]

Winter 2014:

Cut to the girl bleeding on the boy's bathroom floor
again, two days after being kicked out of school for failing
too many classes, one day after moving into the boy's' par-
ent's house. She comes out feeling in trouble for bleeding. She
is bleeding at her own will and hand but feels otherwise. For
the next 10 months, he plays computer games and smokes resin
until 4 a.m.

My love for you eclipses every kind. And according to Greek philosophy there are four brands of it:

Eros

The sort of love that is passionate both physically and emotionally, based on aesthetic pleasure. Typically young love. A typical brand of romance I've had for you always. But then there's

Storge

The sort of love that develops from friendship. Much to do with things in common. Much alike the one that blossomed before a blink for me and you, before

Mania

The sort of love that is obsessive. This comes with many highs and lows. Can be possessive and jealous due to fear of losing

You

And what other than manic love can extend my temper by miles
leave me floating quiet in bed and embrace
like I am under water and influence
so I'm motionless and in bliss; no kicking

Agape

Selfless, altruistic, sacrificial love.

Artists creating passionate odes to the royalty of love is commonplace because love is fucking fantastic

to the point of administering thoughts and decisions with a foolishness at all costs.

I can create odes like this day and nightly, like I do and I've done, and would like to propose: can I make you happy for always?

For A, for ever
68

I'd rip out all the teeth in my head
Would be a spiders' spun lunch to never again
have the doubt stirred about us
See, I'm so tired of fighting like we're over
Of begging you
I'm begging you
to see that I am pouring
My clouds dense with feeling of
only you
Only you
can make it rain good rain, only you
have my love
If you can't have it, no one can. Not even me
I will weed it from the world and save it still
until you'll have me all the way
or

if you are truly done
and we have to be done too
we can keep the car running
so that we can keep going once you let me back in
I'm sorry for literally jumping out while you were driving me
home from work
I didn't know you wanted to go anywhere with this, you never
seem like you do
But now
now I'll sit in two hundred cars in the rain
buckled up and over for you
because I can see leaking photographs
Panoramic glimpses of our future backyard
A pet, a child
Fresh coffee, no scars
An umbrella by the door in a sunny place

Is living bait a survivor in your book?

I still belong to love.

I still love, even with the hook in my mouth

We are both

The catch and go

He said he knows ungodly patience for me

God himself

knows it takes 15 minutes for the spoon to warm

God himself

knows I've spent lifetimes watching him get colder

It is God

and I

who know how to teach him how we build a safe home.

He built me a home and said, "look what I've done for you."

But it was a home of drywalled fear and stiff hinges; no truth lives here.

[chasing, dragons, drinks, drywall]

You could pet me

in a manner that is timid

/heartsick

if to remind me that we

are too tired

to argue

even more than we are too proud to apologize

No goodnight or goodbye kiss

Nothing to do to or for

you or this

[Ravish, miss; text messages]

No more loving voice for you

You could smother me

in a way that is over it

to forget you ever had anything to apologize for

that you spoke to me the way you did

Or I could ask you, carefully, to come to bed

Bribe you with my body

That is only for you

That is only if you

remember what we promised

about going to bed happy

and tangled up

-- growing unfamiliar with your affection

[YOU: ANGRY FOR WEEKS. ANGRY WITH AN ANGER
INVISIBLE AND SCARIER FOR
THAT REASON. ANGRY WITH AN ANGER WITH NO
SOURCE OR REASON. ANGRY WITH
AN ANGER CEMENTING.]

ME, CAREFULLY, SOFTLY AND AFTER MUCH
THOUGHT: I never get to be angry.
And what would you do if I said some of the things you say to
me back
to you?

[YOU: GET SO ANGRY THAT YOU ANSWER INSTEAD
QUESTION THAT I NEVER ASKED.]

You

have been angry for weeks

Your anger is invisible and cementing

I never get

to be angry

When I dare to ask you what you'd do

If I said things to you that you say to me

[YOU: Get so angry and answer
questions I never asked.]

July 23, 2015 - Two Year Anniversary

Soothe you by way of brushing

Your hair and skin

Painting your back

Drawing our way back

through Byzantine wars

Show me where it hurts

Lately you've been trying a lot

Thank you

I know I've been violent

and difficult to get through

I just want to talk about these withdrawals

But you're so avoidant and only nice until I bring it up

I need someone to talk to

but you don't want me telling my friends about our fights

Sleep does nothing for how tired I am.

Top of rum on my tongue

I never meant to start a fire

I never meant to make you bleed

Those things I threw at you weren't really aimed at you

The moon was just full and I was jailed

I did not know I could get that angry

I am supposed to be our peace

For all of the perfect things that I doubt

the shards I drag myself through

and this song we always sing and dance to

A rock and a hard place

Caught between the loss and my mistake

I'd rather us be smashed from our bloody knees to our faces

than to be back to unwanted space to back all day

But otherwise, you're shut up, shut down, bitter boned and
outweighed

It's contagious and outrageously the way your mood is paved

-- just let me touch you

Cut to a park in Manhattan

The sky isn't gray; kids are laughing and playing on in the warm

But the day feels useless and I am too cold to warm you up, my dear

Cut to the end of afternoon

It refuses to get old

Dusk drags like long pants

It's because this day won't end

No, not until one of us says sorry

Cut to the horrible way you looked at me when you found out
I slept with your distant friend before I ever dated you. You
talked to me wrong, but we can't cut to when you face that. We
can't cut to the chase when I'm always chasing you, saying sorry
for things I can't help. We can't cut to the part where you hold
me again because I don't know when you'll kiss me again. Cut
to you throwing my things outside: wrung went my hands, ring
went your phone. You took it too hard but I can't say that. I had
a past featuring other men but I can't change that. Now I will
always be sorry and wrong for it. So this is how it goes: I don't
get to enjoy my days these days for days I had before.

I am learning this is what love is

You should have scared me from it

but you showed me it is very real

-- the fixed heart: within and of itself

[damp feeling, sad kumbaya]

A perfectly made bed covered in perfectly good instruments

Quick, come

here

I need you as you are

Quick, come

here is the way

to music again

Between silence and bowls and Netflix and bowls and trips
to the pharmacy and errands to do and silence and tolls and
nothing to do

Between us between the silence word to word back to back we
are wasting away and wasting our own time
You will tell this story differently

We cannot meet eyes or up
We cannot leave our corners

I
don't
want
to
hurt
you
anymore

You showed me my favorite tea
You're the first person whose complements felt honest to me
You are the only home I know
I
don't
want
to
hurt
you
anymore

We're in love: that could mean we were in or are in love
I am trying to distinguish between these two these days
I
don't
know anymore
Why can't we wake up from this violent loop to a shiver
from a yawn, a gaze
before a long kiss, instead
of slithering out of bed and off
onto smaller and worse things, with no calls attached
only strings at my ends, nothing for my wits
every which way I move
I hurt you

86

Facebook message: Spring 2014

8:22p.m.: I'm sorry

Please answer

8:59p.m.: Think of me as your strong, becoming woman. Not just another girl in the sequence of those who will break your heart and not love you from the moon to break ups to days like these.

9:15p.m.: If I could drive to you and become like

Some voodoo wordsmith

And tell you in one kiss, one hug and one sentence that I need you to see past my flaws and issues

I'll try to work on them, to keep helping me get better until I can be the best for you. So I can be your beautiful little girl, a lady that you're proud of and want to show off can do all those things we had promised week one
x x

I cannot be sad because I am too busy

restlessly and helplessly working a one-woman job of being a cigarette

an inspiration

a good friend

and a heartthrob

And a good bed

and good in it

and good at this

whole game of silencing both of our madness in an unmagic time.

I'm sorry for my other selves

that her strength acts temporary

that her strength depends.

Through entitled breakdowns and sloppy, violent catharsis

they are right.

She cannot fix him.

But she can help him fix him.

Caught in the quiet traffic and snow
and a looping, hollowed "I don't know" because
I am
a tired sad-eyed rag
all out
wearily saying, "Please, I think I need you.
Kumbaya, come by here, here and now."
I can't be that: nagging and losing in domino affected circles
I have built these hurdles

-- losing myself and you, separately and without a chance

Your threats to off yourself feel like weapons and games. Your point to not touch me when I sleep over feels like you telling me to leave.

After you left I thought and sought frantically

for anything you might've left, just so I could chase you with a reason

When I had nothing, there was nothing to do

You were gone and using somewhere

And so I mopped up the whole storm

I shivered the whole night through and through and then

I recalled you telling me I would never wake up alone

Oh, and then I did honey, and somehow the fault was all for me

Something happened to the sleeves

I wiped my nose and eyes on

that I wore my fat and tired heart on

What did I do wrong this time

and how could I feel so guilty and clueless all at once

July 12, 2014

Tonight was my birthday

No one came so you took me to a bar and gave me Xanax

Someone bought me Long Islands

I got out of the moving car

we were on the highway, by the water

You put your gun in your mouth

I wrestled it into mine

It wasn't very romantic

July 13, 2014

We got high and watched Netflix

You were a little nicer today

We didn't talk about last night very much at all

But you went on a quick walk with me so I feel okay

I have

had allegiance to our love,

devotion to its repair

You have

to stay and make up with me

One day

You'll thank some god you were stupid and weak and that you
never left me

A day where I can say my love and promises and love were all
kept

You keep telling me to promise to stop storming out

to give up my disappearing act

You are mad I keep breaking

I know I run away like a coward

I swear it's just that I'm one of those who would rather leave
then be left

(know that I stay like a coward too)

Summer 2015:

Cut to all of their clothes in the trunk of a Hyundai Elantra being shipped to Los Angeles.

You can't sleep unless I'm here, that's what you said

And when you do, you're scared

Cause you've got big dreams, but even bigger nightmares

I know this

And I know I help you get sound sleep
Please touch me back tonight

First night in California

Thanks for the flower, babe. Audible and oh, so musical are the violet waves of light in our shared life and within it's flux and webs and tension... We have shared the same muscle memories, nightmares, and now, dreams come true. And now, kingdom come. To have trailblazed cross country with my king/guide/ medicine, to be preparing to grow grounded here, to live once again an ocean from Japan, up the road from Mexico, in Californian winters and her *laniakea* Junes...

The sense of overdue belonging -- with you, right here -- is thrilling but humbling

[cake, angel, pumpkin, honey]

Paint each other to sleep nightly and

both your chest and offers to keep me

look sightly on my mouth

Can this please be what everyone's referring to as heaven

Can this please be what everyone's referring to as heaven

melatonin pressed on khaki skin

hair to hair

from your smile to our

mailbox

our child to our first date

a cheers to all our future driveways

to no more street parking when we come home from date
night

to infinite date nights

because I can count on

(all my petals)

seeing our end

This must be

(what everyone's referring to as) heaven

I paint that chest of yours to help you breath easy and deep

After all these years, you're finally asleep

Paint your arms to alleviate the rotting retention

brush your scalp to let that beautiful brain breathe

and paint your everything to see that

you wake up and hear me

harder that

you're everything

That I love you much more than I could ever attempt to explain

Far more than I could promise

Miles more than you think

I want to you to grab me by my baby teeth

I

by your peach fuzz

our innocence keeping us

instead you tether me

only to jettison

only to Key West and California

only to leave me unravished with passion

how could you come to me for pleasure without loving me

how could you come to use me like this

still

how could I let you

for no reason more than

my equally selfish attachments to your body heat and embrace

to where your peach fuzz used to be

to the way you shave at my teeth

then kiss me anyway

November 21, 2015

With Thanksgiving around the corner, I'm excited to be with your family. Our family. I am grateful baby, that you are kind. You are maturing into the best kind of man. Your patience is intelligent and honest, expanding and evergreen. You appreciate me more than ever. You fight for me. You care enough to hide from sad poems and big fights.

November 22, 2015

We've had some remarkable fights these past few months...but
if there's anything to recall from this fall is that

He is GOOD

[endless volition to start again]

I don't remember who I was. I know I took too many, and I know I threw whatever I could grab. And when I was cleaning up the glass from the bathroom floor, I realized I had thrown my two new vials of perfume. One that said Relax and the other that said Breathe.

Once I

kissed you I could not

remain angry with you or God

And God knows I've tried

And you know you lied

when claiming oblivion

to your being

my weakness and tissue

The gods know I've cried

these truths to you

with my knees on the grits on the splitting floorboards

on the house on the street your parents stay

One day

all of your selves will

catch and keep me for good

You will hold me there, til the end of the while

then you lay me down alive

upon sheets of recess

to play before rest before soft blades and the dewy silence

beneath the lot of shade of all the little ways

you finally love me back all the way

February 2016

I am

dripping from mind to chest,

In blood and words

because I cannot unveil the woman's way to tell you

"That was mean.

I am upset.

I do not want to play."

That is a girl's way

a child's truth

the pure and innocent truth

and when

I take to the pen

you do not like this

you get defensive and see it as a weapon

Well maybe it is

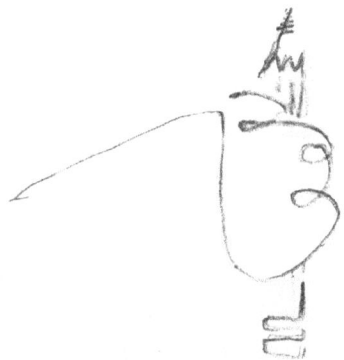

Well maybe you just had a bad day at work, maybe you are having another bad month

I take to keeping it buttoned inside but you tend to notice the stretch of the chest

The popping of buttons and the bats of the lashes and a wave of a question

The rearrangement of fingers

The tucking of truths

A dry wave of affection to hide in

Closing Winter 2016

I wish things with him were just increasingly beautiful or ever-rotting. But that's the thing:

We are months

with no sun

Then we are perfect

weather

We are the calm

Then the storm.

You've started ordering the little green ones from Romania. There's no return address and the stamps are pretty.

I haven't cared to take drugs in two months, despite you keeping pills around. Although the anxiety is bad, your greed makes avoiding them easy.

Instead of taking those, I've taken to dancing when you aren't here. This is how I can be myself out loud. It feels so cathartic that when you get home from work --harshly telling me to turn my music off, prickly and attacking in four billion little ways -- I flee. I cry behind the apartment complex til the music in my headphones in louder than my sobs. They slow to a sniff and a trot and I dance. I dance until the delivery driver and the neighbor's cat and the landlady across the way are staring. I dance until it is itchy and cold out. I dance for if I stop, my throat will start to stop, and I will go back submitting to what you say I've done wrong that day, apologizing myself into the kitchen.

We are breaking up soon

Innocence was stolen

Innocence was stolen

We robbed ourselves of three years

so we could wrestle with flames we flung

Innocence was stolen

So we could starve ourselves on the ground of these hearts

A meadow to a dirty public restroom floor

-- soulmate, expired

[hell, stealing, steal, stolen, falling from grace]

All you gave

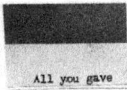

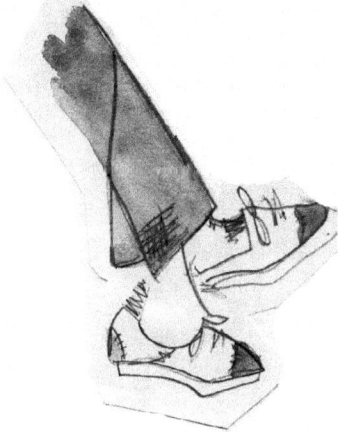

III

But I will miss how our fingers would sleepwalk toward each other's waists and collarbones. I will miss the great width of your warm feet on mine, your cooking, the way the fit of your lips and arms would convince me I must not be meant to leave. I will miss the sunny vintage blur on the lens through which I remember our first summer. You fed me endless wine and poetry and MDMA and lovely naps and lovely cocaine and passion fit for gods. For cinema. For true love. I will miss that night in Mexico and all moments like that, when you were an honest lover with eyes for me. For what was right in love with you, wrong in love with you, right in front of you, oh how I would have built with you these dreams to come true, these truths to come truer, these vows to come up in fights where all I need is to lay with you

I miss already

the patches of (manning) hair on your baby skin

Our love does not will to last

but the echo of it will

and God, did we shout

[cut to when the birds fled at our cries

flying the distance to match

how long it took us

to flee from this ourselves]

Cut to my first bath after you

I am too weak to speak.

without you I am alone

without you I am alone

I cannot unlove you

I am boiling myself clean

And there is water in my heart

And the sludge of us seems to go

on and loop unto itself

I could pull again

Miyazaki's village of bikes

out from under this wet scar tissue and

I'm not for anyone else

I'm not worthy or lovable

You've ruined me and now I'm only fit for you

I'm sure you were right many times

And it aches to imagine that

one day someone will love you

where I didn't earn you

I'm sorry I acted so stubborn and ugly

But don't go falling in love without me

You videochat me and I force myself angry and busy

so I can't hear my phone from under the water

I miss you more than I've ever missed Mom

you were my entire family

you were mine, assigned til Death

I miss you more than I've ever missed Death

Death didn't do us part

I ruined the best thing

I ever did have

I miss you and your call

You once called me a coward

and that rings now

as I dip under a bath full of fear

my body is wrinkling gray

Every body is a holy land

mine was yours

but nothing but dry soil without you now

Yours was my Babylon

a byzantine
empire
of things I'd recognized
but did not know in this lifetime

I chased
that aged feeling
like a tail on fire

I swelled
with love for you, fought for that love
like a dog

I suddenly reaalize that you apologized before

but I couldn't hear it until you left

Your voice sounds lovely from under

the water and weather

I should have said sorry hard

and more often

Why did I always hide from you in the bathtub

But why did you only join me twice in two years

You never really wanted to get clean with me, did you

Was it me and my mania

Because I told you not to love me but I still kissed you all I
wanted

Was it me and my violence, my mother's

Did I take enough responsibility for it

We hated the way it stopped and pretended it was leaving

Forgets something and storms back in

I am done bathing

Blurred, tiny body but taking too much space

Water too low to keep me warm

Thank god I lost those pretty green pills in my robe pocket last month

Or I'd care to not shiver to sleep

The water has grown colder than I and I

am a mop in May and may

as well sleep to death in warmth

Because I deserve at least that:

the basic right

of warmth (I just won't imagine it your warmth)

I sculpt mindlessly

wet the bed with my slow body

the bed that still belongs to us

Soap still on my pruned skin

But I will not care to imagine this warmth belongs to you

-- unconscious healing

Maybe we can fix this. I will stop bringing up the time you pushed me out of your room, I will stop bringing up Courtney and Tori and Riley in my head, I will stop. I'm finally ready to change. From your ears to our old front door, god, I want to change. From your smile to our old mailbox, I want to plant trees with you. Have food fights and make a good living. Adopt that bunny, write those songs. God, I want to change.

I've been meditating and looking for free therapy. I've done some research on bipolar disorder and manic depression. I think I inherited my mother's temper and her methods of dealing with anger. I think I can't stop talking when we argue because I was silenced throughout my childhood. I think I'm ready to accept your love without denial. I'm sorry. I'm sorry. I haven't slept or eaten or gone to work. I'm staying on Taylor's couch. I want to come home.

if we each have

the breeze

smoke signals,

maps.

multidisciplinary   ventures of soul.

the   t o   o   l   s

to meet again

I need to be the best version of myself possible

for you

or at least the girl you fell for

This past year, you've only drank and complained

You need to remember that things are beautiful

that you are beautiful

I need you to try

I need you

I will out do the old me that loved you better

I will be patient and consistent and loving and cooperative and mature and responsible

That night I took too much

and I took to hurting you

Your hand and head bled

I saw red and blacked out

I don't remember anything but my screaming

You told me to leave for the first time

And I know it's over for good

I made a playlist today. It's a chronological telling of a feeling.
The sound of catharsis for those who feel in wrong. The feeling
when you've lost someone for real this time. The thesis of it is
something like: Sure, get to healing; make yourself better and
keep the better even if you can't keep the someone, yeah.

But for now, evil-shedder, be a pillow-wetter as you mourn
your romantic innocence and capacity to love like a child.
No one told you your demons were contagious and you never
made a leash. Choke the demons with that leash and miss him
all you want. You will forget but for now

for now

for now:
cry so violently and thoroughly that the demons dart away.

It's been two weeks and I haven't changed clothes, showered or gone to work. I've covered this sweater in snot and my face is swollen from the crying. My sobs are heavier than all I own, which sits on Taylor's balcony. I sit on her couch. Two weeks. How long is this part supposed to last

I have stopped caring about my hygiene, my femininity, or music. I listen to the same 12 songs. I make colder suggestions to my friend in need, for my mug is empty and speckled with dead fruit flies.

I'm realizing you resent me for not making much money

You are always the one to fill the fridge

I was $50 short for rent once and you told your parents it happens all the time

June, 2016

Cut to a train back to our town

It is almost midnight and I am running a little late because someone jumped in front of the Amtrak. She is dead and took awhile to be cleaned up.

I sit, layout my makeup and order wine. I do this differently, more confidently, than I would have while I was your girlfriend. I got a modeling job and make much more money than when we ended things.

Two months ago you told me to leave and now you tell me to come back.

So I try to look very good to make you sorry or something.

However, no matter my charm, I'm still nervous at dinner. You still run the show. You are much sweeter now, and have almost mockingly taken on the role of being a gentleman but endearingly so.

Catching up is very informative and dramatic in a dry way. You say you are not doing well. Your health is poor and so are your excuses for not changing your ways. You even relapsed - very, very badly.

You haven't changed

You get drunker than I do, I have to drive, a car accident, cut to black.

Somehow, this wasn't even the point.

And you want to get back together

You take me out to cry over sushi

In the car, you say things like,

"You are my war paint."

"I want you to outlive me

and live off my labor

I want you to be comfortable before I go

And I am going to go"

"I would marry you tomorrow,"

you say. "In fact, fuck this

Baby doll, let's go right now

Mexico is twenty minutes away

We could be married in an hour

I will cheer up and go on walks with you every day

Baby girl, please

I hope I die first so as to ensure you read every last word of my writings

Toward the end, you read so little

Then tried to defend you were still interested in me at all

The waves in your hair are ripples in a frozen creek that leads to the end of an overwhelmingly nostalgic movie, your scars more like birthmarks, your leg hairs like an old bed of that soft kind of grass in front of a grandparent's home. You have always been home. Since before you were mine, no matter how dangerous it was to know you, I felt safer with you than I ever did growing up or with my parents.

Because before you held me I knew your arms, like the forks of a windmill when it's hot, or the lock on a cradle when nightmares come true, would keep me safe. But what I didn't know was eventually your arms kept me from myself; then they would cradle me to little avail and then none at all.

I didn't know you would bring out the worst in me. I didn't know the perfect medicine can be so bad for you in the end: so expensive, so hard to swallow and like the child-resistant pill case, harder to open up

-- a medicine cabinet of issues being cleaned out

You were my fellow horseman

You were in earshot as we pulled up to the battle

The warrior separating us was killed by you, I didn't notice

You before, I didn't notice

Her before

As more than a handsome woman, I always

focused on my own fight

Didn't know we were fighting the same, didn't know we were
after an apocalypse or that we would be apocalyptic or that you
were two saddles away, sir

Your sword was so pretty.

I knew not what to say

or how to hold mine

So I tucked it behind me and when I fell from my horse, you
had to catch from the tip of it and carry me home by it and
hold it close to my neck

As I made your horse sick with my disease and myself homesick
by fathering you

I think I'm happy without you

Discover holy, discover angels, faraway messages, priests, angels,

proximity of a God, window of light, sun, yellowish,

*sometimes light is harsh and unwanted

*sometimes new love is unfamiliar and rejected

*sometimes you get a second set of parents

they will try to heal you and you will runaway

you will twitch and fret and bark at a loving touch

mistaken for the ways you've been touched, the ways you've
been loved

and loved

others

how you loved yourself

a new love;

I imagine them to smell and touch and feel in ways xeroxed from you

In sepia sunglasses, memory-lensed, blood-cleansed blurs

a backyard swing, an easy pull of gravity

no pushing

A good shiver, a home

apple pie, apple, Adam and Eve, grace, gold-colored,

afternoon sun, hands, angel, a God, a father

light, light

[PAN TO A GOD BEING EVER PRESENT DESPITE OUR SIN.]

tomorrow sun, strong legs, glared, clear messages in leaves, Mother

light, light

In a perfect world, people would break up just until they grow enough to get back together. But in this world, things need to be immediately fixed or otherwise replaced in order to feel at home.

Healing doesn't come in throngs of shed relief from these heavy and, henceforth, impervious hearts, but instead it comes from exhaustion; after the person trying to heal has cried out all the torturously romantic memories that you can't erase out of a home

> like when you taught me how to say "pe-tri-c(h)or" in French and I taught you to say it in English. If you don't remember, that is the smell outside after it rains and a shit metaphor for where I'll live after you

> like these past twenty-something months I've spent trying to teach you the order of the seasons

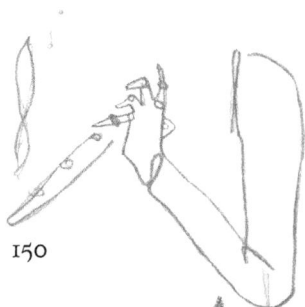

> like last week, when you decorated me: neck to stomach to
eyelids to hands, in kisses that would make a monster drowsy,

In a perfect world we would remain loving
in a fairytale where The Velveteen Rabbit and Peter Rabbit
elope in summertime, in summerland

MID-SUMMER: A TIME AND PLACE where you and I initially fell in love under my dorm room bed, so inviting yourself over that first night was like stabbing me because we couldn't stop gushing in disbelief at it all and it was lovelier than all the metaphors we came up with to describe our love and each other.

(like the way I graze the Earth while you pave it and the way my back's scars totally look like constellations to you)

A PLACE and A TIME

A time when everyone's delight is in loving like Greek gods

A place where it turns out those broken up with were way bet-
ter off

A time and place where rabbits play and take breaks until they
grow enough to get back together mid-summer, mid-summer,
mid-summer

But now, and here, in this time and place

people taking breaks eventually decays

into people breaking up, and into two parts:

One person doing the replacing, be it with illegal, romantic, healthy, or hollow substances,

be it of the times or places that rang loveliest

Be it as they play of the villain in every break up

song the other plays for the next few years

and the other person?

It's all heavy chimes with no wind

the other crawls out of bed after two consecutive sleep cycles

trudges along like long texts on long nights

or sad sex

That other person is left with the impressive skill of inducing themselves into all that blissful sleep by crying and masturbating manically

to reels of memories of lovemaking, cuddling

That other person also possesses the impressive skill of managing to only cry for an average of

two hours a day because he, well she, well I'm only awake four

the impressive skill

of only staring at "send" but doing nothing about it and being

able to laugh at these living cliches since it's easier if it's felt in

masses in this world

of cloudless, reasonless rain for dry soil, I can't find other reasons to grow besides you.

Because perfect worlds consist of perfect times and places and once upon a perfect time and place, I was bored in bed with you.

And now, in this same world, my heart's hollowed and splitting.

I want to make a one-woman fairytale, I want to get more stumps of hobbies, another five than I have already

I want to disallow the sight of your name to be so vampiric and you from being the same

I want to keep revising my feelings and desensitizing angelic things about you into normal things, flaws even

I wasn't born to love you, no, not until I met you.

I may have the worst back a woman could have at my age

Will likely die with my debt unforgiven

Have no parents or appetite or use in the kitchen but if I could
have anything

all I'd beg for is for something to (please) give me a glimmer
of a chance
to stop loving you

because I'd rather have gone to bed beside you and your indif-
ference
than being dropped on my neck
almost as much as it's dropping breadcrumbs
to someplace, sometime worse
Someplace, sometime, someday better
where I can let people in because I'm emotionally decent

[Pan out to a wide shot of a dirty looking girl tiredly sobbing in her laptop, getting in bed with the sun, with the dust of shut blinds dancing in, riding on rays of light, sometime after 4p.m., someday after I left.]

Swollen with a love for you

I was doomed to be ruined by you

and I loved it for the first part and the most part

Oh, Aaron, I was throbbing with true love for you

that love was made for you

Made for healing you

I am begging you to try with me

Knees bent like the corner of a page:

Can't you read me anymore

Can you not see how I wither for you

We would always stay

run but not go, chase or throw

then hide

We would always go

Red flag, red flag, red flag

White

please explain:

Why am I always crying when I write about you?

Why did you procrastinate on valuing me?

We could have been everything?

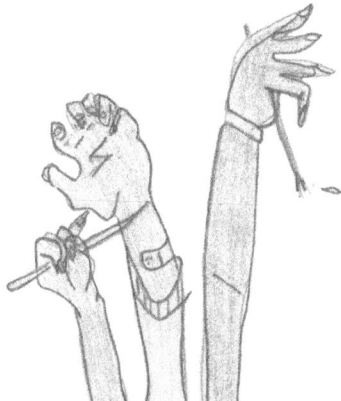

The fight last night left my whole body

Sleeping on the floor, quailing

My love last night left my whole body

-- out of body, out of love

-- out of reasons to stay

I found that if you imagine a place to be haunted, it will be.

Figuring this out meant understanding that if you treat someone like an animal, they will behave as such.

I can imagine myself into failure,

all slammed doors and none knocked on.

I can imagine myself into a meadow

where I'm granted the calm, then the storm,

but I can't imagine the storm away.

To repair this meant a required renovation of my perceptual lens:

this meant

making a mosaic of the parts of me that were rended and shattered again.

This meant something near impossible

So what does it mean

when I beg him to rub my back - "fine, where does it hurt?" -

And when he finally does, his hands hurt me?

My head hangs like a chandelier

(I'm ashamed that I'm not obliged)

I quietly think, "You are rubbing, technically and visibly, the same way as usual -

your thumbs in circles, but it hurts. This hurts."

So what does this say? About his hands or about my back?

I don't know what it means when fears draw like a flooding bath

as I realize he loved me differently before:

gratefully

and so deeply,

I'd imagine the ocean floor before we fell to sleep.

He was the ocean contained: a deep, leaking mass, plugging itself up to be loved

his edges adored by strangers but his depths unimaginable

and I, I was another sea, distant but hushing him to sleep.

He shoots, he's sore

But then I come in, stage left, like an angel sent at the right

scene and I love him through and through,

to a healing degree.

He throws storms at me and I stay

He makes a monster of himself and I say,

"I will love you, even when you won't."

My exercised endurance makes me tired yet lovable

suppressive and but a mattress of a woman:

he comes to me to make love and rest and restart

and so we did.

Clean now, he was ready to return the love and patience

but just as I was ready to stop suppressing -

"I would draw my curtains just as he was trying to hear me
I'd run, he'd chase

"I'm done," I'd say

but we never were

And so we richochet

But we adore these shifts in each other still

There was never doubt in these

We were as comfortable in each other as the ground
wrapped around the core of the Earth, quake included

Feet on sand on land included, sea to sea with feeling included

So comfortable I thought I ought to die with him mine;

So divine was this love that I'd often thought,

"There should be stars for this feeling."

But just as there should be a proper way to wage a war

a fit manner in which to lose lovers after you've run dry of
fight in you,

are we finally done because

oh, I could smell the emptiness where his warmth used to be

I am more a violin chair of a woman now, setting him up to be
judged, picking through the show for where his warmth used
to be

I mean what does it mean when he thinks I've been working a
war on him for weeks

but I am just trying to focus teary eyes and stuttering heart on
where his warmth used to be

What does it mean

When I've already lost him in feeling, but not yet in title?

What does it mean when I am letting 1 a.m. think for me

2 a.m. drink for me

Still waiting for him to come home from the bar at 3

when I've been feeling like 4 a.m. on a weekday

and he's been more and more like 7 p.m. on a Sunday?

When my heart grows comfortable with feeling as heavy as a planet

as heavy as my crying body when I wait up all night

And he is just as comfortable with leaving us as we are

What does it mean when I find myself imagining the ocean floor, but it looks dry?

There was a leak somewhere and now he's gone,

he's drained and so I've already lost him

and even if his words say he's here, he's not

and when I lie alone between 11 p.m. and 3 a.m., he's not

and when I lie with him between 2 a.m. and 9 a.m., he's not still

he is close but cold

we are stretched history and empty bed space

we are quiet dinners and no pillow talk.

So I find myself imagining the ocean floor

And believe me, baby, I want to be all stars and champagne bubbles and sea foam

But I found that if you imagine a place to be haunted, it will be, but this is not to say one can imagine a heaven for oneself.

Nor a silver-painted lining on all nine dream clouds per cycle
of fought-for sleep

Nor a bloody, stitched-on sheepskin lining to every new pair of
wings

These do not make for a true heaven

branches

Under

their perfectly warm bodies

You may not force heavenly fantasies to exist atop hellish circumstances without paying mind or a stepping stone to reality.

A true heaven is not imagined into existence, but remembered.

I want to build something new to wear out

something new that resembles that heaven

I want to be planting seeds and cutting trees

and trying to hush my sea back to me, back to sleep

But I can only cling to the memory of us like wet leaf to window

I am still hurling darts at the sun

aiming to make a big bang of feeling

to feel love like that again

I miss you, yes

but I'll never let a love in again

that looks anything like yours did

Yet how will I know when you came running in so pretty

Organizing a war

on my wounds

as a tribute

to your hand

How did I let you make me feel so much lesser and so unworthy

[basic, love, forget basic love, remember basic love]

Your love grew cold quick

turned comfortable so soon into things

I'm angry now, realizing

how badly I'd like to hold the old me when you wouldn't

with abuse

the abuser usually does not know they are being abusive

you are signing, blindfolded

for a condo with no key

The landlord is the muse is the hero

Feeding you dreams

Only to guiltlessly work a slovenly violence

Picking at your bootless gauze til they can spot your wounds

Stretching the gash and preying on a soul unmade

but to their knowledge, they were just trying to help you or sell
you something

I want to know why you let me live besides you

cleaning our home and messes

Trying

to want to make love

Make a home of us

when you weren't in love with us anymore

Like a jail in the wintertime

being sailed through on a glass bottomed ship

I'm at rest, although it's chaos I'm amidst.

Like a finished battlefield's deathcount

collecting stardust for new lives now

that the sharper winds have blown:

my sadness was that of a manic street preacher

dipping frantically in an emotional palette

only to keep crying to the world in water

in clear color; no salt, no sun

I granted you a favor you should have never obtained

And that was to trust you despite your history and poorly pitched dream

I fowarded you reigns

That we had no business seeing

As anything but mine

I love you to this day

After all you put me down for I'd still say

the waves in your hair are ripples

in a melting creek

Your ugly scars are aesthetic to me

Your leg hairs like an old bed

And you will always feel like home.

Until that day, years from now, that we grab coffee to catch up.

We will talk about how it really looked like we were supposed to be together

really felt like

we were supposed to be.

How

since before you were mine

before I knew how dangerous it was to know you,

we were always home.

and I felt safer with you than in my mom's house

Before you held me, you arms were home

They were the cradle and the cradle's lock

They were the nightmares and the dreams and the mobile, too

The car and the crash

They were the sickness and the medicine

But I didn't

know

the perfect medicine

could be so bad for you

or so expensive.

A little song is not short and a big song is not big

I belong to love, in spite of tests or sin

I still love you; I love you so, you
little, big song,
you grand old thing
shiny new toy, sweet little face, big heart, big mouth, big head,
little teeth
you little ocean
you big idiot, big blanket, big love
lux sunset, salt of everything I know
you
the balm of my heart
the bone and point of it

And although it didn't sit right with us

our love still stands, still runs

And no matter the target

I would still hold your guns

My last calls to you were battle cries

Those emails, my white flags

Off key, I thought maybe I need you

Need as in to survive

I've wrote you too many poems

You wrote me maybe two songs

once I tried to leave

Well this is my garden song

A sonnet to myself to sing,

"I need you in past tense,"

In tune

[red flag, red flag, red flag, white]
[born, pillar, dust, settling, trust, no settling]